GW00771199

This notebook belongs to

Published by Bamboo Umbrella Books

Printed in Great Britain
by Amazon

84299320R00059